I0450658

# 101 Ways To Heal The Hurt

# 101 Ways To Heal The Hurt

## Dealing with the death of a loved one

By: Deborah Stefaniak

Writers Club Press
New York  Lincoln  Shanghai

101 Ways To Heal The Hurt
Dealing with the death of a loved one

All Rights Reserved © 2003 by Deborah Stefaniak


No part of this book may be reproduced or transmitted in any form or by any means, graphic, electronic, or mechanical, including photocopying, recording, taping, or by any information storage retrieval system, without the written permission of the publisher.

Writers Club Press
an imprint of iUniverse, Inc.


For information address:
iUniverse
2021 Pine Lake Road, Suite 100
Lincoln, NE 68512
www.iuniverse.com


ISBN: 0-595-26978-8


Printed in the United States of America

# 1.
# One

Know that sadness, loneliness, fear and anger are legitimate emotions after a death.

# 2.
# Two

Crying should never be thought of as "breaking down."
It is simply our response to begin the process of healing the pain.

# 3.
# Three

Boys and men feel grief just like
women and must be told and shown that
it is all right for them to cry too.

# 4.
# Four

When someone dies, we remember things
we said or did that we regret.
We should remember that it is human
nature to get angry and say things we
really do not mean. Forgive yourself.

# 5.
# Five

Let this loss remind you that the secret of life is not to be the one to finish first, but to be the one to enjoy it the most.

Don't live speedily, live abundantly.

# 6.
# Six

It is experiencing grief, not denying it that will ultimately guide you to healing.

# 7.
# Seven

Death is not a punishment, but a necessary phase in the cycle of all of life.

# 8.
# Eight

You cannot expect to put a time limit on grieving. Understand that it is God's natural process of healing.

# 9.
# Nine

Understand that it is not God's will to cause you pain, but that somewhere there is a greater plan at work.

Learn to trust Him and release your anger.

# 10.
# Ten

Be mindful to be patient with yourself. Take each step of grieving moment by moment.

# 11.
# Eleven

It's OK to miss the one who has passed. Talk to them in your dreams by simply stating before sleep that that is what you wish. (Give it time-several days)

# 12.
# Twelve

Remember it is not up to you to fix a wrongful death, nor is it "your fault" that your loved one has passed.

# 13.
# Thirteen

Pain is the result of resistance to change. Although change is the only constant thing in the universe. Let the pain go. Death is beyond your control and in line with universal flow, even though you may not be able to think of a valid reason now.

# 14.
# Fourteen

Believe in your guardian angel.

No one of us is ever alone.

# 15.
# Fifteen

If you were the one meant to die, you would have. No one qualifies as judge as to whose time it is.

# 16.
# Sixteen

Realize you are the only one who will decide when and how you will close the wound and begin again. Don't hold yourself back.

# 17.
# Seventeen

Embrace any remaining issues you have with the one that has passed, feel them, understand them, and then let them go.

# 18.
# Eighteen

Breathe deep, letting a little of the pain go
with each breath.

# 19.
# Nineteen

Try to focus more on the living with you
now and learn of course time is short.
Decide today not to let that time pass
between you and another without sharing
your heart.

# 20.
# Twenty

Understand that guilt develops naturally
from grief.

# 21.
## Twenty one

Know and accept that it is not "your fault". Don't torture yourself with the "if only" or "what if" game.

# 22.
# Twenty two

Realize God has not deserted you.

Don't desert Him. Begin a closer relationship with Him today.

# 23.
# Twenty three

God didn't create us to be alone.

Call a friend, or family member. Talk about the good times.

# 24.
# Twenty four

Talk with others if you feel shameful or
guilty for a death somehow. Talking about
it will help you release it.

# 25.
# Twenty five

Accept your loss, the death and pain.
Then rearrange your life to fit the present
reality.

# 26.
# Twenty six

Do not hold yourself responsible for someone else's actions or decisions.

They were here to learn their own lessons. No one can truly know what they may have been.

# 27.
# Twenty seven

It is our childhood fear of abandonment and rejection that holds us back from communicating with others to heal.

Cross that line and begin the process.

# 28.
# Twenty eight

Death makes us feel frighteningly insecure and fearful that everything and everyone will be taken away.

Voice your concerns with a spouse or friend to allow these fears to dissipate.

# 29.
# Twenty nine

Write a letter to the departed. Write your feelings down on paper.

When you're finished, burn the letter, throw it in the lake and release yourself and your loved one knowing you have been understood.

# 30.
# Thirty

Try not to shut a spouse out. Realize you both may be grieving. Support each other.

# 31.
# Thirty one

Allow yourself time to connect again. Meditate, walk or just breathe deeply connecting with your inner spirit and strength.

# 32.
# Thirty two

Remember above all that we are spirits first, and spirit never dies.

# 33.
# Thirty three

Allow your grief to become an avenue for your growth spiritually with God.

# 34.
# Thirty four

We all have chosen experiences to go through as spirits. Consider for a moment that this is what this soul chose to go through in order to evolve spiritually.

# 35.
# Thirty five

Death is most often a choice made on a spiritual level by the departed, not an accident waiting to happen.

# 36.
# Thirty six

Feeling guilty over something that has passed will not change it.

# 37.
# Thirty seven

Ask yourself "what lesson am I learning from this experience?."

# 38.
# Thirty eight

Know that whatever happens in life you are still going to be OK.

# 39.
# Thirty nine

God doesn't make mistakes. Be mindful that YOU still have a purpose on this earth.

Go on to fulfill it.

# 40.
# Forty

Remember, you cannot control all situations. You can, however, control your reactions to them.

# 41.
# Forty one

Be mindful that death in reality is truly a new birth in spirit in the next phase of life.

# 42.
# Forty two

Remember you are never alone.

God is always with you.

# 43.
# Forty three

Be mindful that our loss reminds us of
our own mortality.

# 44.
# Forty four

The mind is the divine connection.

Talk to God everyday.

# 45.

# Forty five

Remember to look beyond this life into the scheme of all things that are ever changing.

When a rose has lost all of it's petals, they
fall to the ground and die,
Mother earth embraces them,
never asking why.
In spring the rose is born again,
this time new and bright,
Rejoicing in the life it's chose,
Shining in God's light.

# 46.
# Forty six

Embrace and accept the changes now in your life.

# 47.
# Forty seven

Accept that there is a time for everything
to pass.
Accept there is a time for everything to
live.
Where one is present, so is the other.

# 48.
# Forty eight

Accept those things you were able to do.
Accept those things you did not do as
those things that were not supposed to be.

# 49.
# Forty nine

Although our loss makes us feel powerless, let our knowing of a plan for all things make us feel powerful.

# 50.
# Fifty

Give yourself time. Moment by moment
to heal, and day by day.
Step by step, forgiving you along the way.

# 51.
# Fifty one

Know that you will always carry with you
the heart of those you lost.

Know that this IS real. Let it warm your
soul.

# 52.
# Fifty two

Know that you make a difference in everyday in every choice, every word, every expression you show to another. Their healing may begin with you.

# 53.
# Fifty three

Review your thoughts and mental attitudes. Focus on hope and triumph, not despair and defeat.

A shift in thinking may open your door to serenity.

# 54.
# Fifty four

Invest ten minutes into a walk to lift your
spirit and reflect.

# 55.
# Fifty five

Put on your headphones and listen to music to defray your nerves and soothe your soul.

# 56.
# Fifty six

Employ the therapy of laughter. Laughter is a direct antagonist to anger, fear and depression.

Rent a funny movie or call a friend with bad jokes.

# 57.
# Fifty seven

Volunteer to help others.

# 58.
# Fifty eight

Become a child again.

Do something you loved to do as a child.

# 59.
# Fifty nine

Change your environment.

Change lighting in your workspace or move your furniture around.

# 60.
# Sixty

Accept the hard moments knowing they will pass.

# 61.
# Sixty one

During the holidays remember your loved one through a symbol.

Burn a special candle at Thanksgiving dinner or hang a special Christmas ornament on the tree.

# 62.
# Sixty two

Find a unique way to remember your loved one at the holidays by using the money you would have spent on a gift to help others in need; donate to hospice, needy children, soup kitchens.

# 63.
# Sixty three

Read for encouragement.

Go to your local library and arm yourself with inspirational and self-help books.

# 64.
# Sixty four

Feelings of loss will leave you fatigued.

Respect what your body is telling you and lower your expectations of yourself for a while.

# 65.
# Sixty five

Let your tears come and go.

Cry when you need to. They are natural emotions and when expressed freely help you feel better.

# 66.
# Sixty six

Let your limits be known.

Don't let others coerce you into activities you feel will be unpleasant.

# 67.
## Sixty seven

Healing from the hurt is not unlike the healing from a physical injury.

You will go through the process as you must, and you will heal.

# 68.
# Sixty eight

Think journey.

When you lose someone you are in a process that will take you from one emotion to another. Trust in the process of recovery.

# 69.
# Sixty nine

Inability to resume "business as usual" is common. It's important to know and recognize this is normal.

# 70.
# Seventy

Know that there will be good days and bad days.

# 71.
# Seventy one

Remember your grief is individual to you.
Not everyone's grief is identical to yours.

# 72.
# Seventy two

Reach out and seek others out to fill the void—whether it's going to a show or joining a support group

# 73.
# Seventy three

True life is flowing movement and unbroken wholeness.

It is what we in our ignorance call life and what we in our ignorance call death, separating that which is merely different aspects of that wholeness and that movement.

# 74.
# Seventy four

Create a garden in your loved one's
memory.

The time with nature will allow you to
center and connect again.

# 75.
# Seventy five

Keep something special from the one you lost to remind you of the good times you spent together.

# 76.
# Seventy six

Don't try and go it alone.

Realize you may need and accept help.

# 77.
# Seventy seven

Nurture yourself with a bubble bath, good book or pick up a new hobby at least once a week.

# 78.
# Seventy eight

Create a "comfort quilt" from fabrics from the clothing of the one you lost for you or a child.

# 79.
# Seventy nine

We can't escape or hide from grief, we must walk through it.

# 80.
# Eighty

Light lavender, pine or rose scented
candles to uplift your spirits.

# 81.
# Eighty one

Take a long shower. Close your eyes and let the water run over your head visualizing as if the water is cleansing your soul and washing away all of your grief.

# 82.
# Eight two

Close your eyes and picture your loved one. Communicate to them all of your thoughts and everything you wish to say.

Allow yourself to cry. Repeat daily as necessary until there are no more tears, only joy.

# 83.
# Eighty three

"When one door closes, another opens; but we often look so long and so regretfully upon the closed door that we fail to see the one which has opened for us."

—Alexander Graham Bell

# 84.
# Eighty four

Sometimes we feel as if our "safety net" is gone. Learn to trust your inner voice now and become dependent upon yourself.

# 85.
# Eighty five

If you have lost "approval" from the one who has passed, be mindful it is only your approval you need seek now.

# 86.
# Eighty six

Realize you are not a perfect being
(you're human) and love yourself
unconditionally. This may require some
time. Be patient with yourself.

# 87.
# Eighty seven

Realize you may begin to close yourself
off from others, just to avoid further hurt.
Be mindful of this and know the heart
was made only to love.

# 88.
# Eighty eight

Remember that forgiveness is most beneficial for us.

Should there need to be forgiving for something the departed has done or not done, doing so will only help you to heal.

# 89.
# Eighty nine

Just for today be joyous with that beauty
that surrounds you. The trees, flowers, or
a blanket of snow.

# 90.
# Ninety

Center your thoughts on learning to live.

# 91.
# Ninety one

Remember it is little by little, moment by moment that transforms us.

Patience.

# 92.
# Ninety two

Realize that all you have to deal with, is this one-day.

# 93.
# Ninety three

Even though you may confide in others,
you may feel that nobody understands
what you're going through.

Dwelling upon your trouble will only shut
out what is there to be enjoyed. Don't
deprive yourself of the little things that
may bring you joy.

# 94.
# Ninety four

Realize that suffering does not stunt, but
spurs growth.

# 95.
# Ninety five

Celebrate those you love while you can.
They are not ours to keep; they are only
lent to us for a while to keep us company
on what ultimately seems to be, for each
of us a solitary journey.

# 96.
# Ninety six

Send messages via thought waves and dreams, prayers and meditations.

# 97.
# Ninety seven

Pay attention to the coincidences of hearing your departed's favorite song, or smelling a familiar scent.

All things sent to you to let you know that they are indeed OK.

# 98.
# Ninety eight

Realize the connection in love with the one who has passed is not broken by their exit from physical reality.

# 99.
# Ninety nine

You may receive dreams, visions, flashbacks or daydreams that seem real. They deliver messages of comfort you may need to hear. Be assured this is normal and very real.

# 100.
# One hundred

If it seems a part of you is missing, it is.
No one enters our lives that do not effect
us in some shape or form. Some more
than others. Accept this and try to fill that
space with the knowing that for the time
you were together you are thankful.

# 101.
# One hundred and one

Remember that it is ultimately you who will choose how to live each passing day.

0-595-26978-8

www.ingramcontent.com/pod-product-compliance
Lightning Source LLC
Chambersburg PA
CBHW031230280526
45784CB00004B/1512